The Wise Men brought gifts to Jesus.
Can you finish drawing this Wise Man?
Draw a line from one number to the next.
Color the picture.

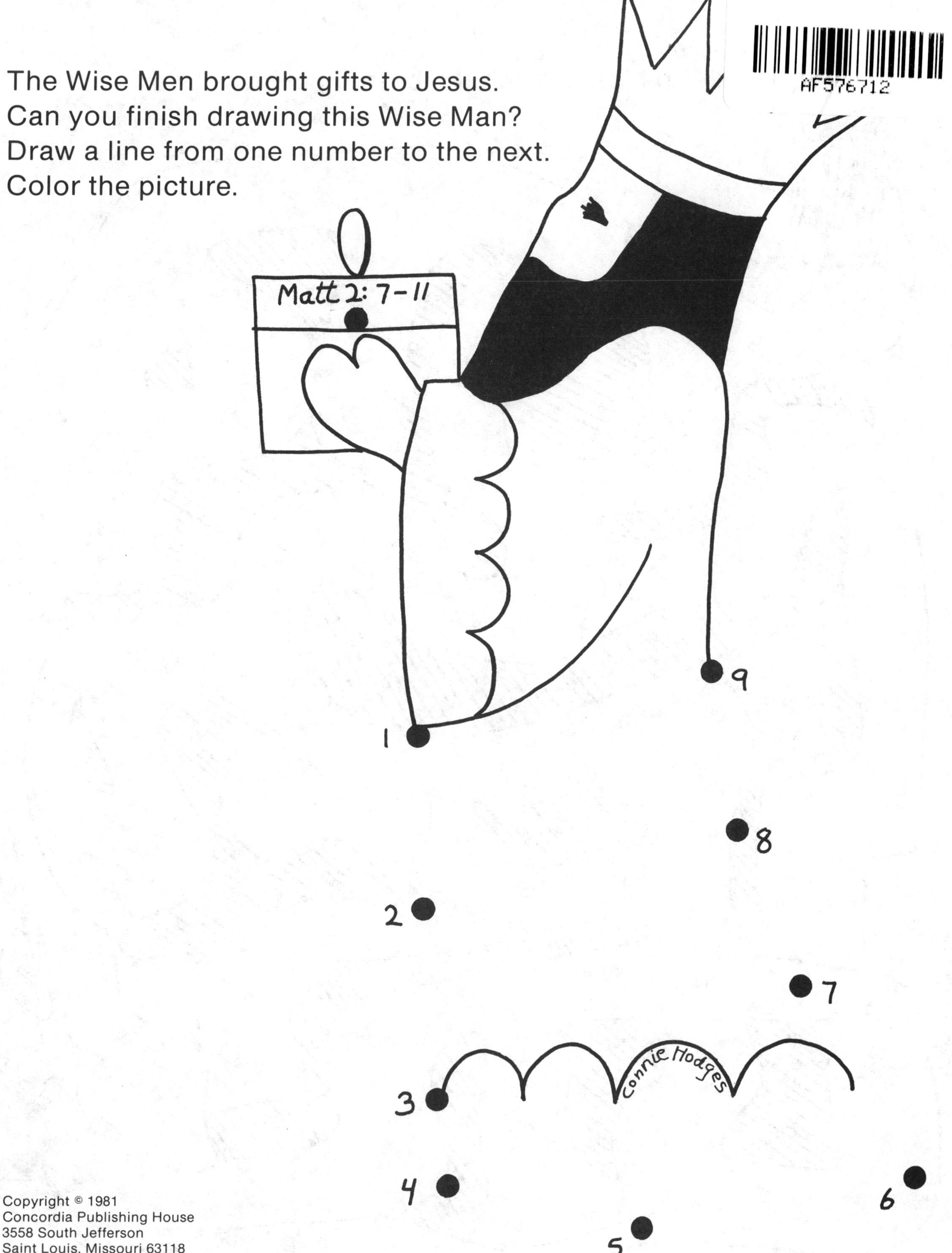

Concordia Publishing House
3558 South Jefferson
Saint Louis, Missouri 63118

Manufactured in the United States of America

Help Moses reach the burning bush.

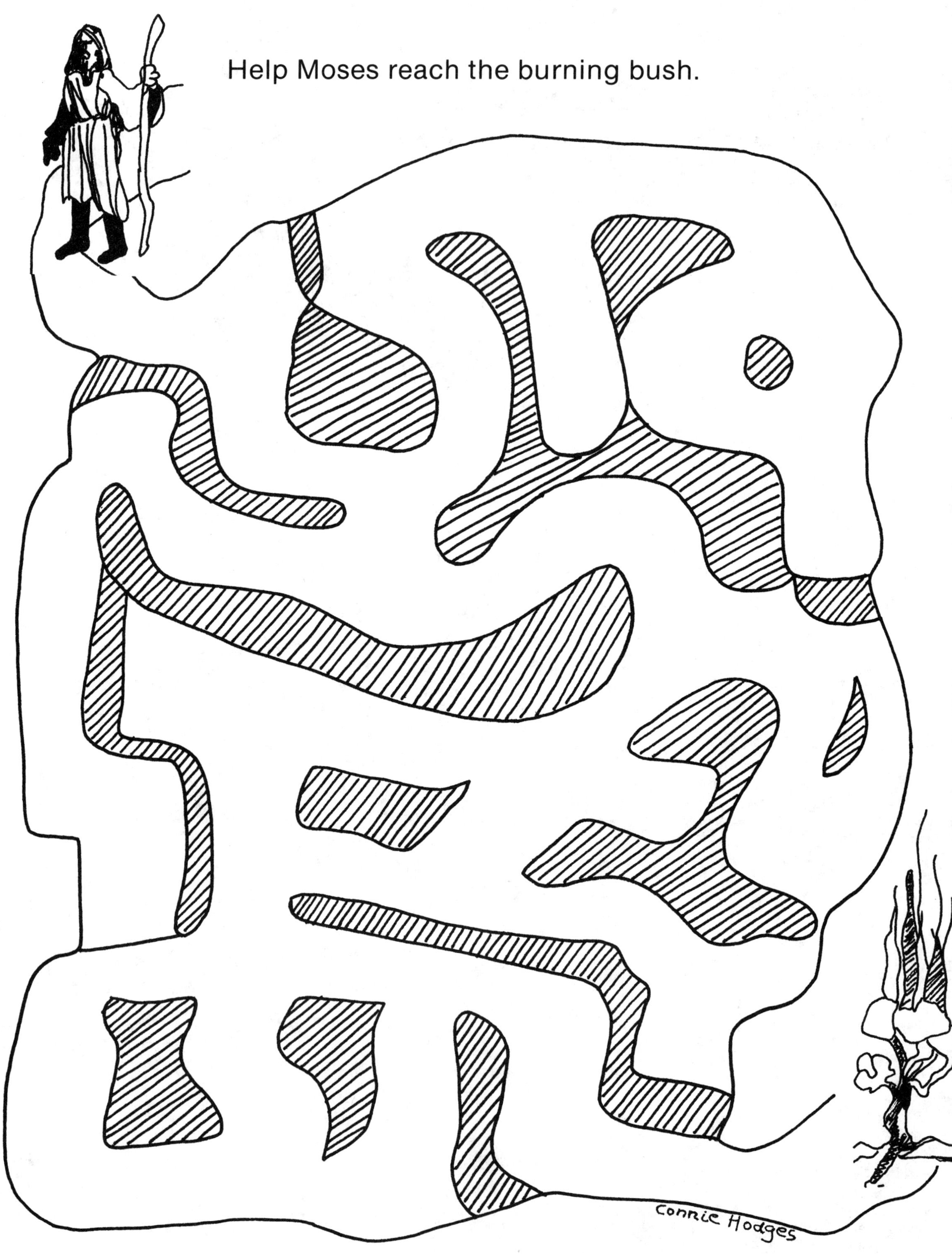

ARK
RAIN
NOAH
Gen. 7:1-5
Fill in the blanks.
R N
R
A
Connie Hodges

Fill in with colors the shapes that contain a dot.
What do you see?

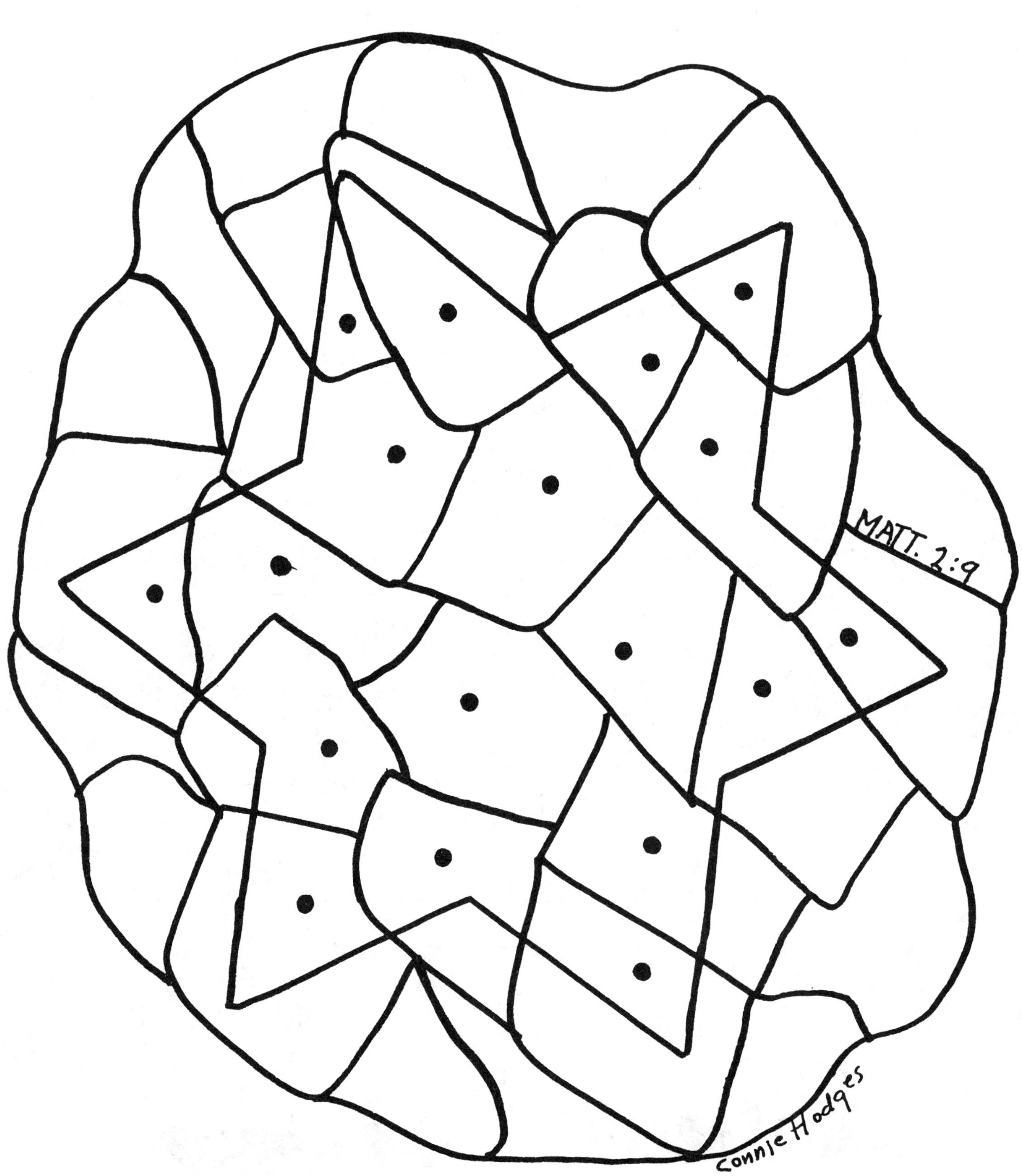

Help the Wise Man follow the road to Bethlehem.

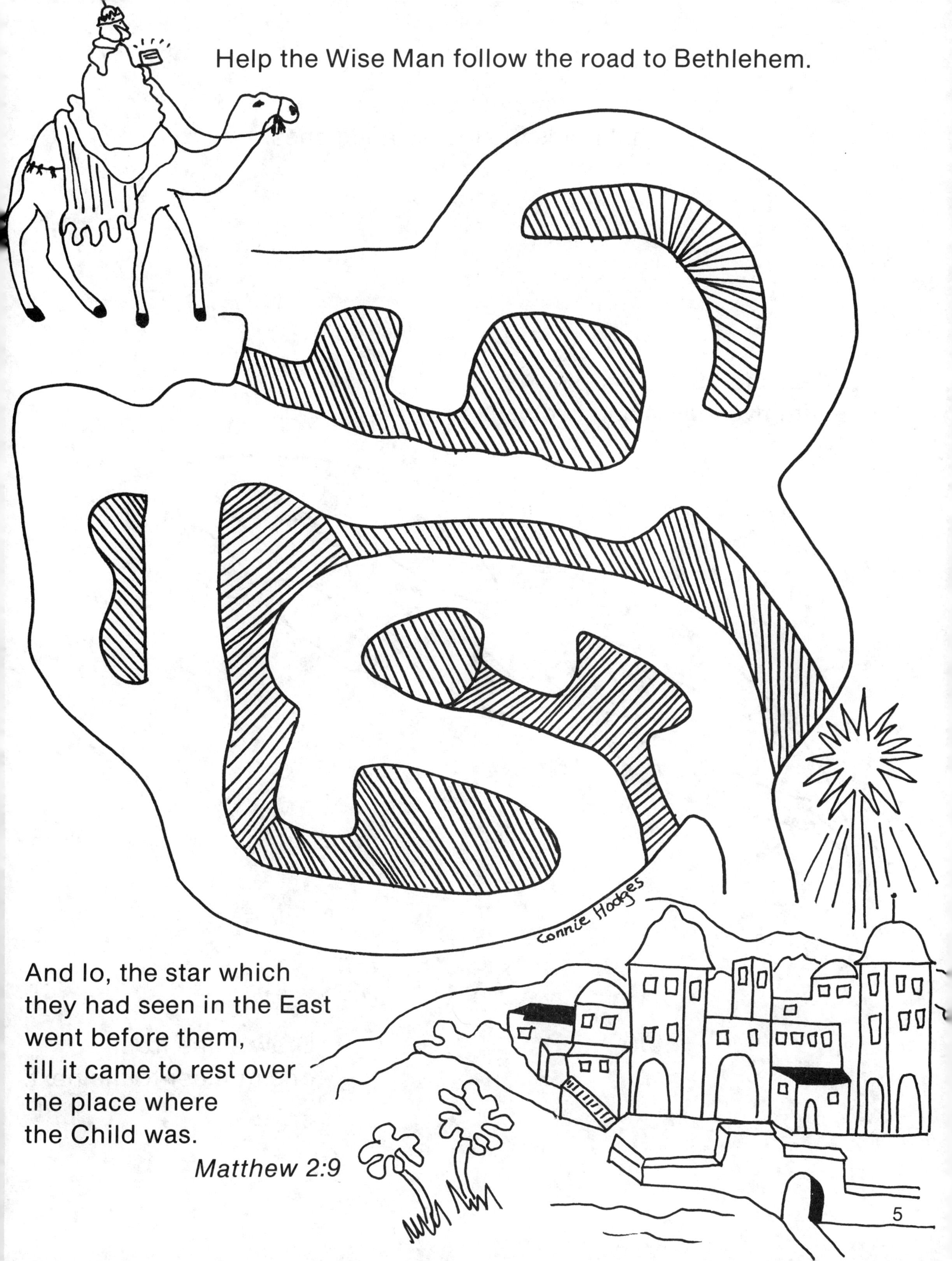

And lo, the star which
they had seen in the East
went before them,
till it came to rest over
the place where
the Child was.

Matthew 2:9

Complete the basket
that holds the loaves and fishes.

Jesus fed 5,000 people
with five loaves and two fishes.

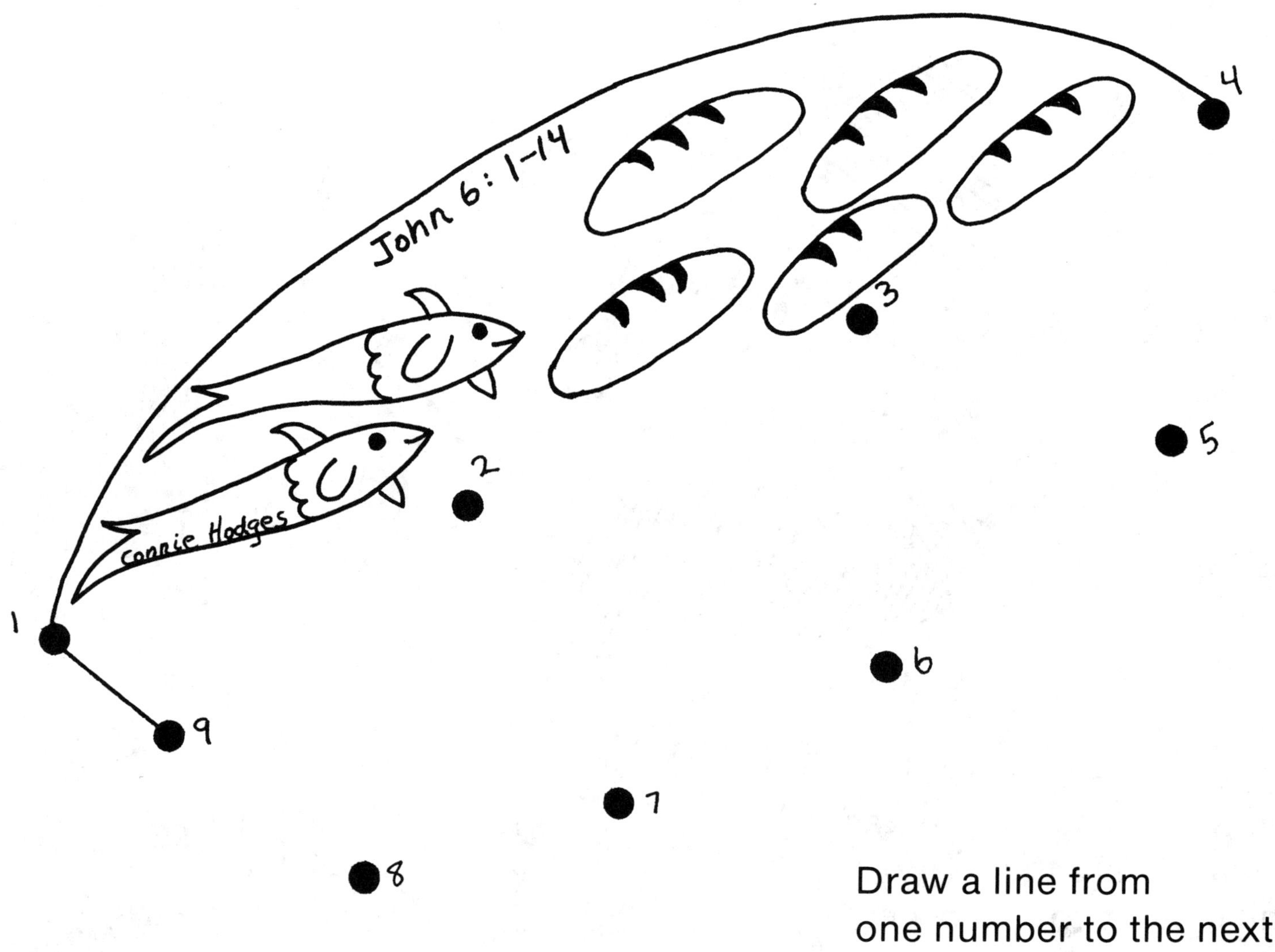

Draw a line from
one number to the next.

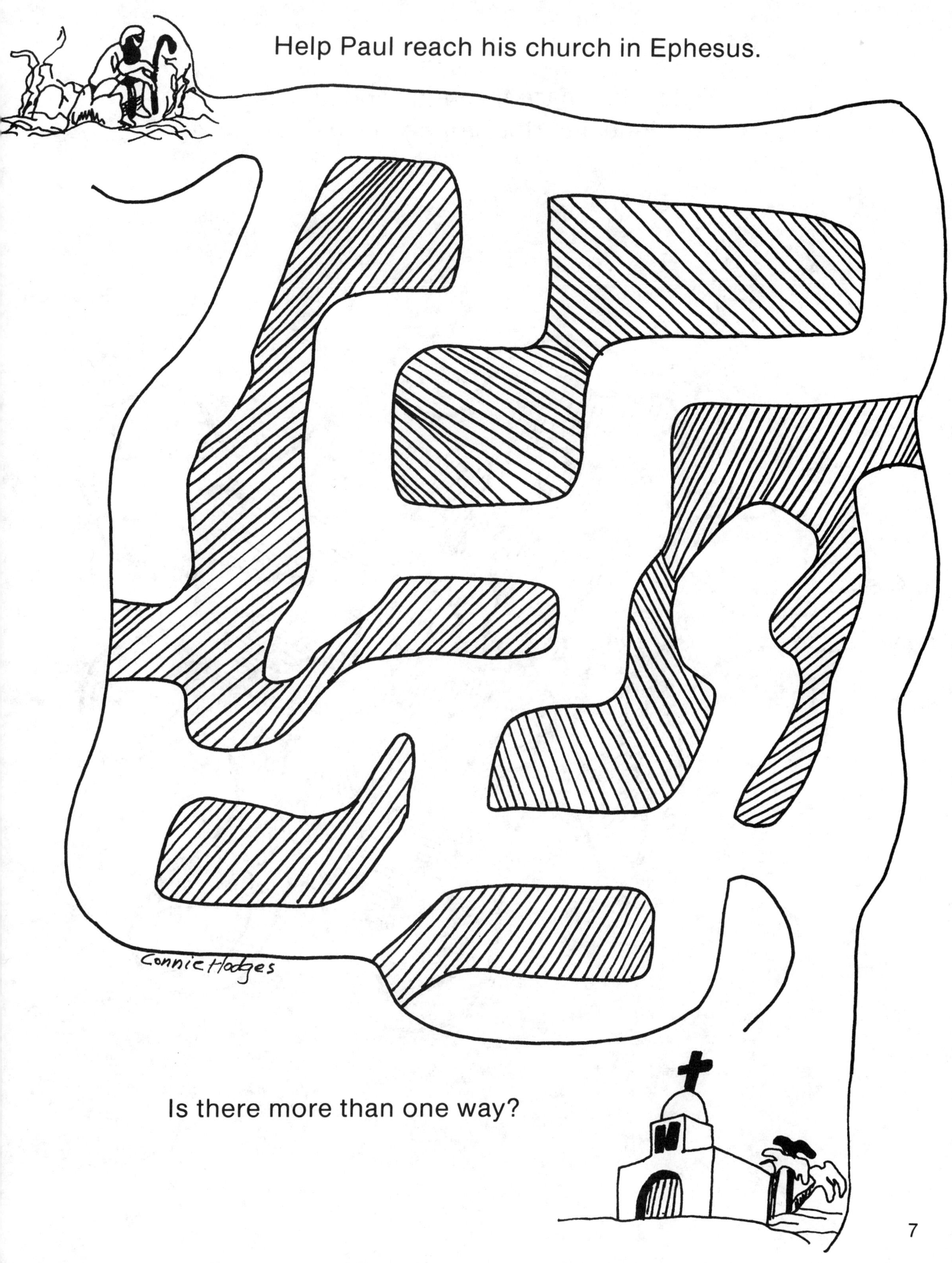
Help Paul reach his church in Ephesus.
Connie Hodges
Is there more than one way?

Follow the maze through wind and gale;
Find a partner for each whale.

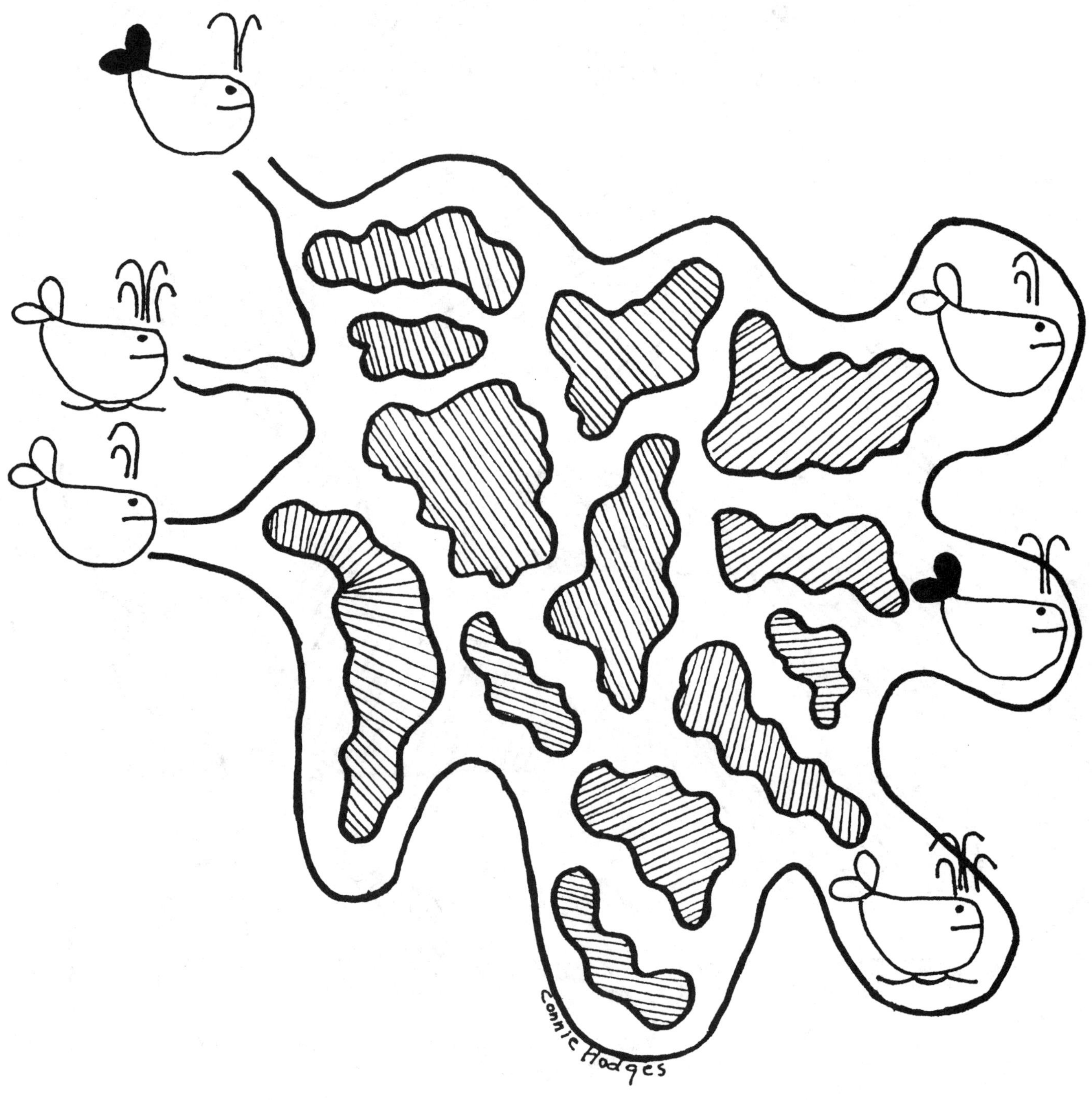

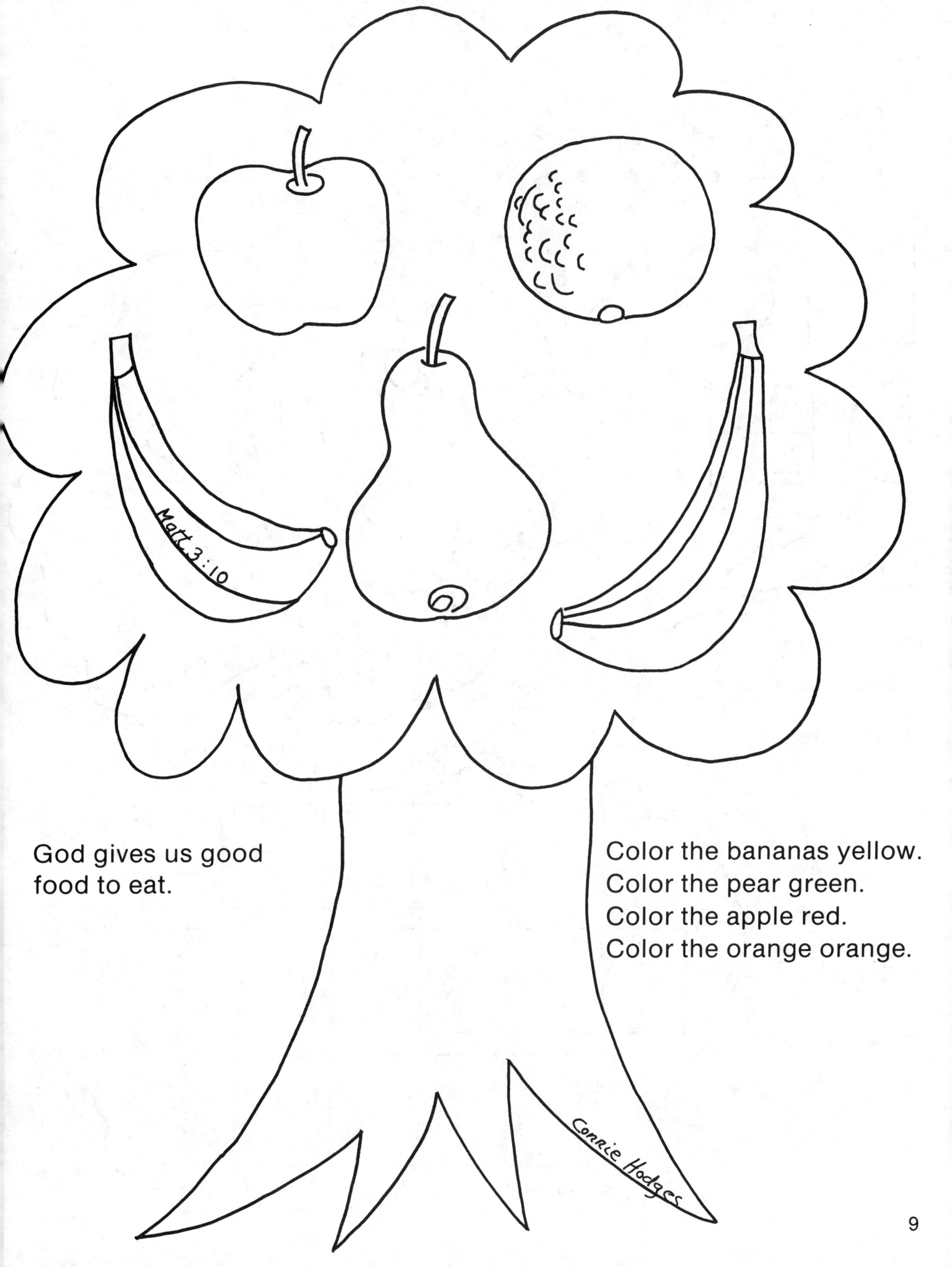

God gives us good food to eat.

Color the bananas yellow.
Color the pear green.
Color the apple red.
Color the orange orange.

Fill in the blanks.

God told Eve not to eat the fruit
of a certain tree in the Garden of Eden.

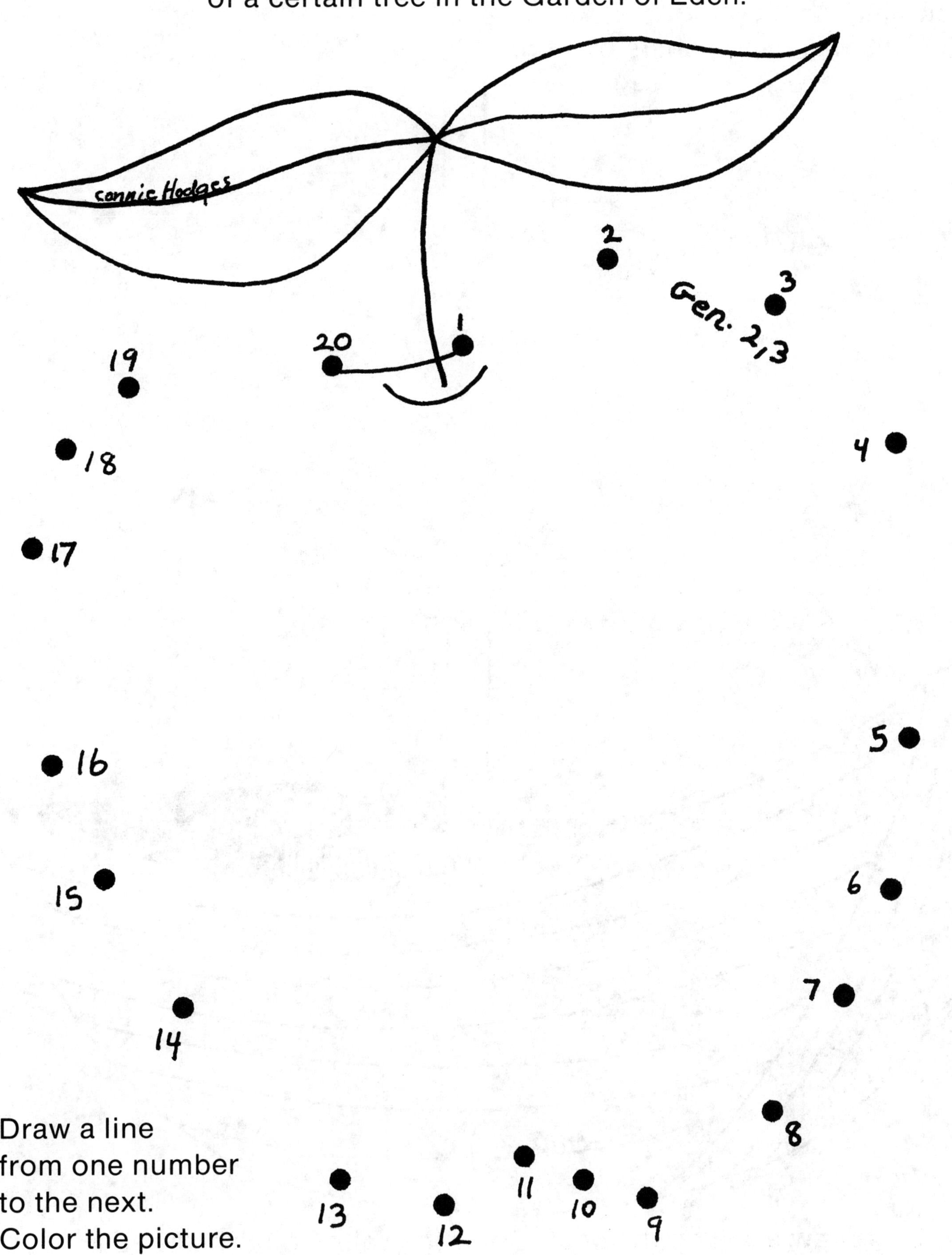

Draw a line
from one number
to the next.
Color the picture.

Jesus said: “Follow Me,
and I will make you fishers of men.”

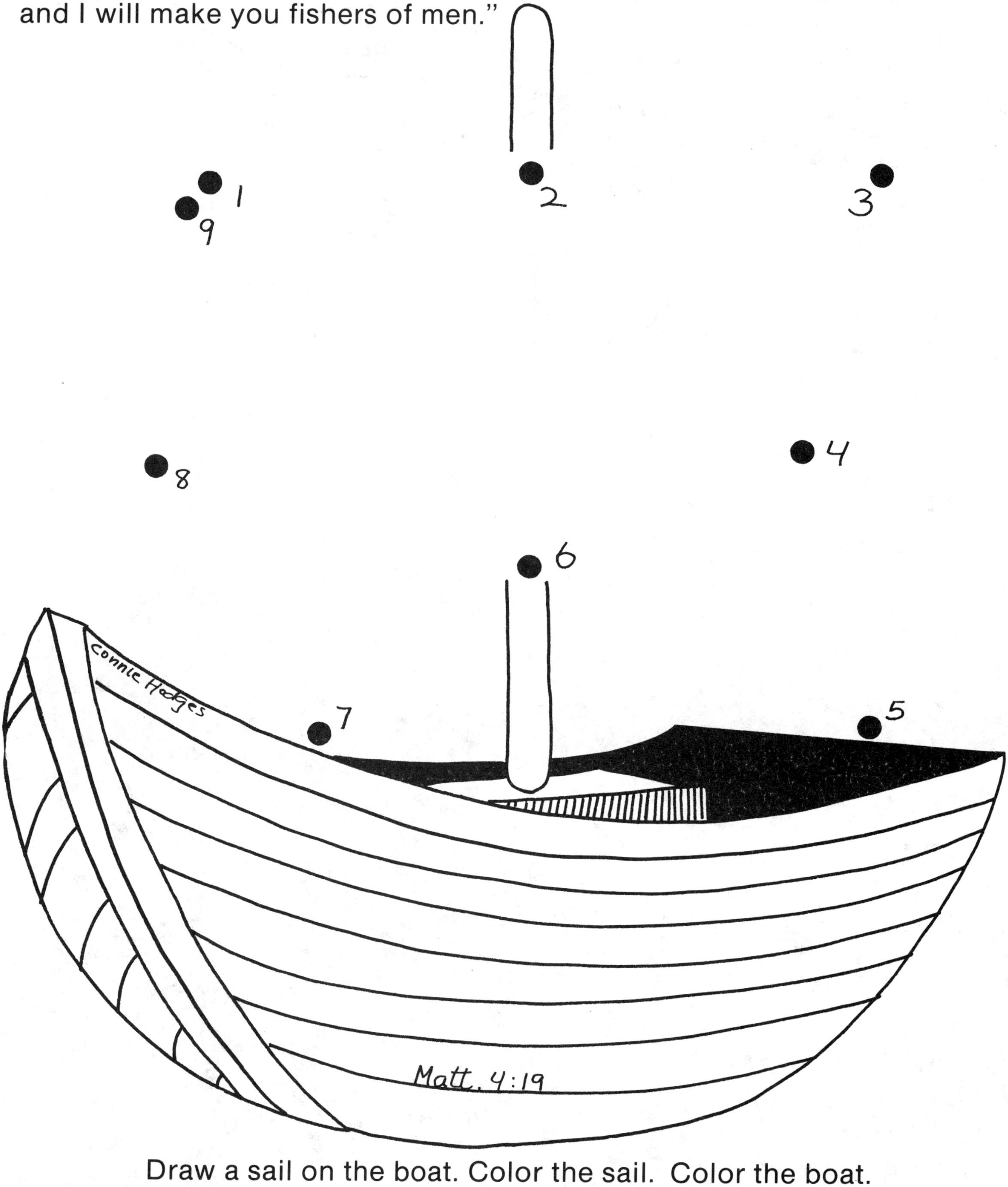

Draw a sail on the boat. Color the sail. Color the boat.

Fill in the spaces that contain dots.

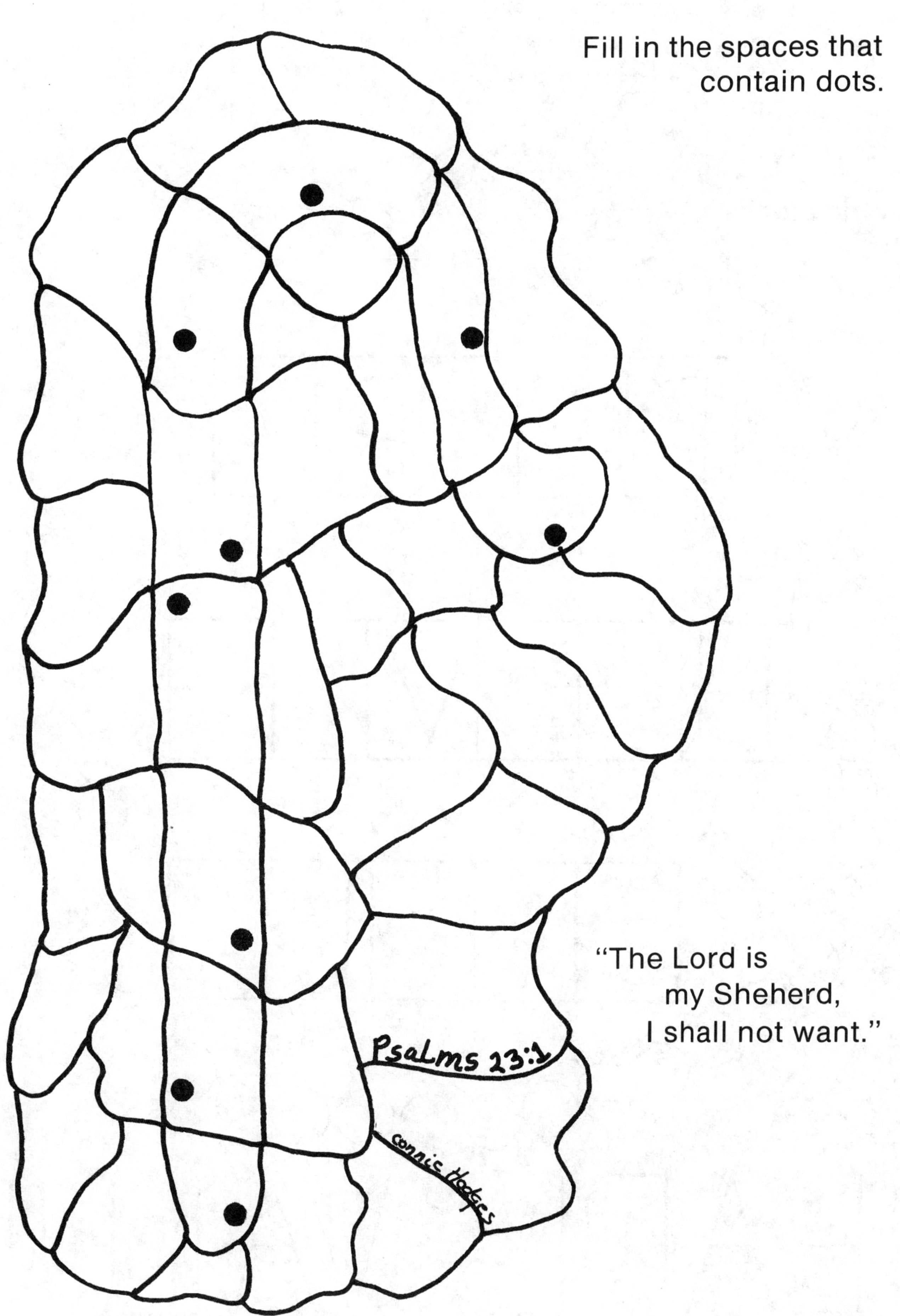

"The Lord is
my Sheherd,
I shall not want."

HEAVEN
Fill in the blanks.
Matt. 13:45-46
P R
H V
U
Connie Hodges
PEARL VALUE

In Bible days the Egyptians
built pyramids as royal tombs.

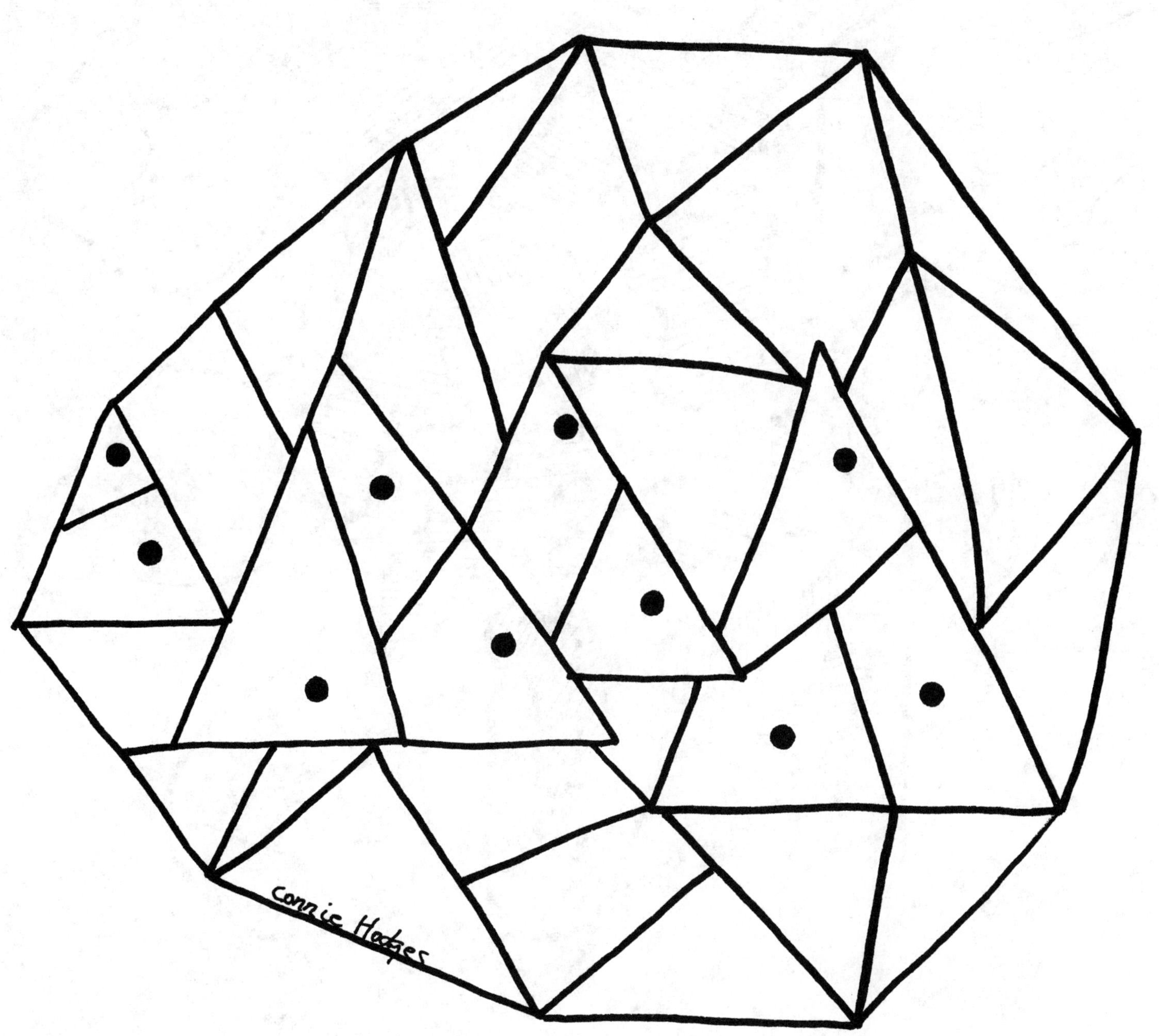

Color in the spaces that contain a dot.

Help each little snow-white dove
Find a mate—its own true love.

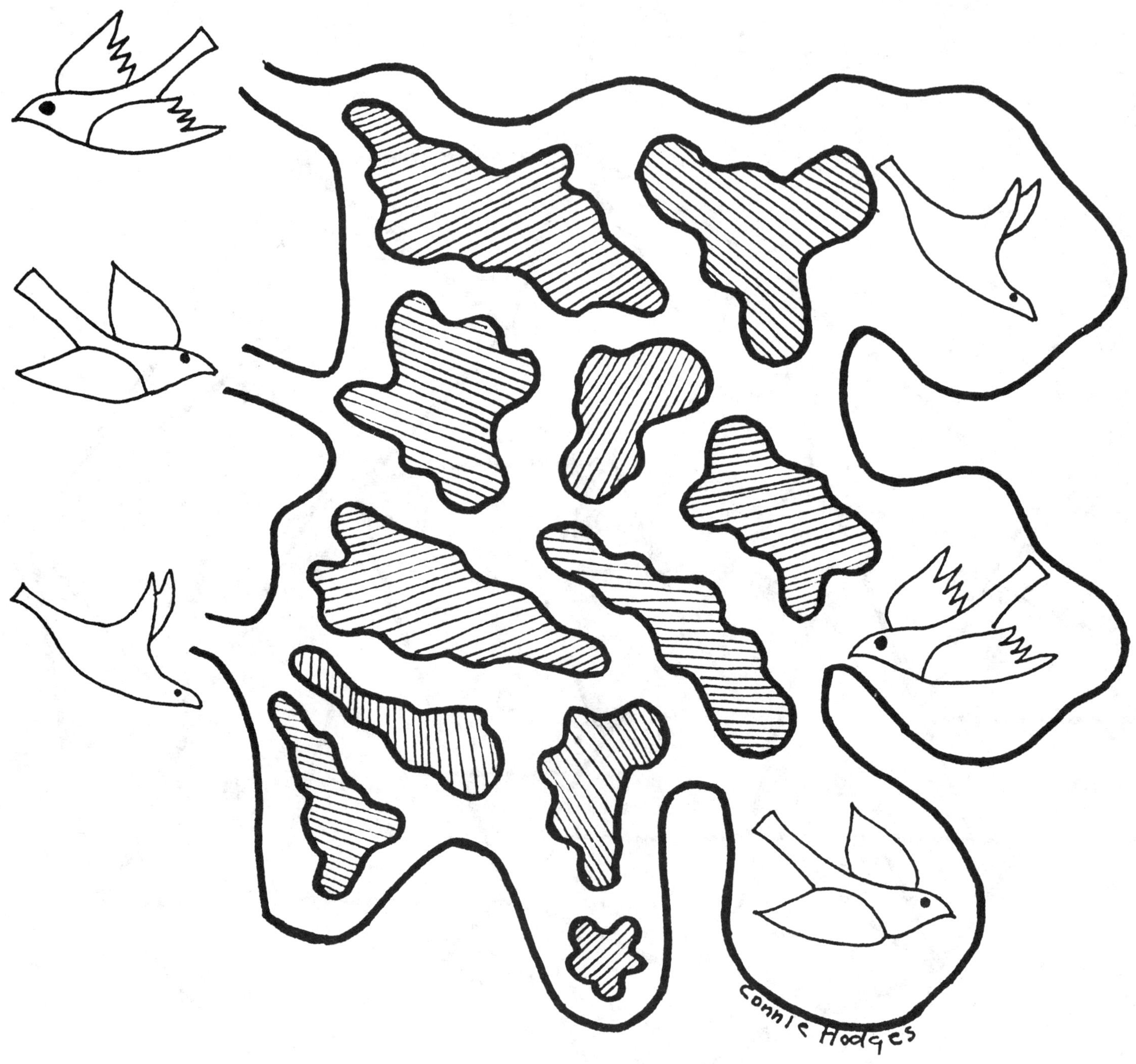

Color the shapes that contain a dot.
What do you see?

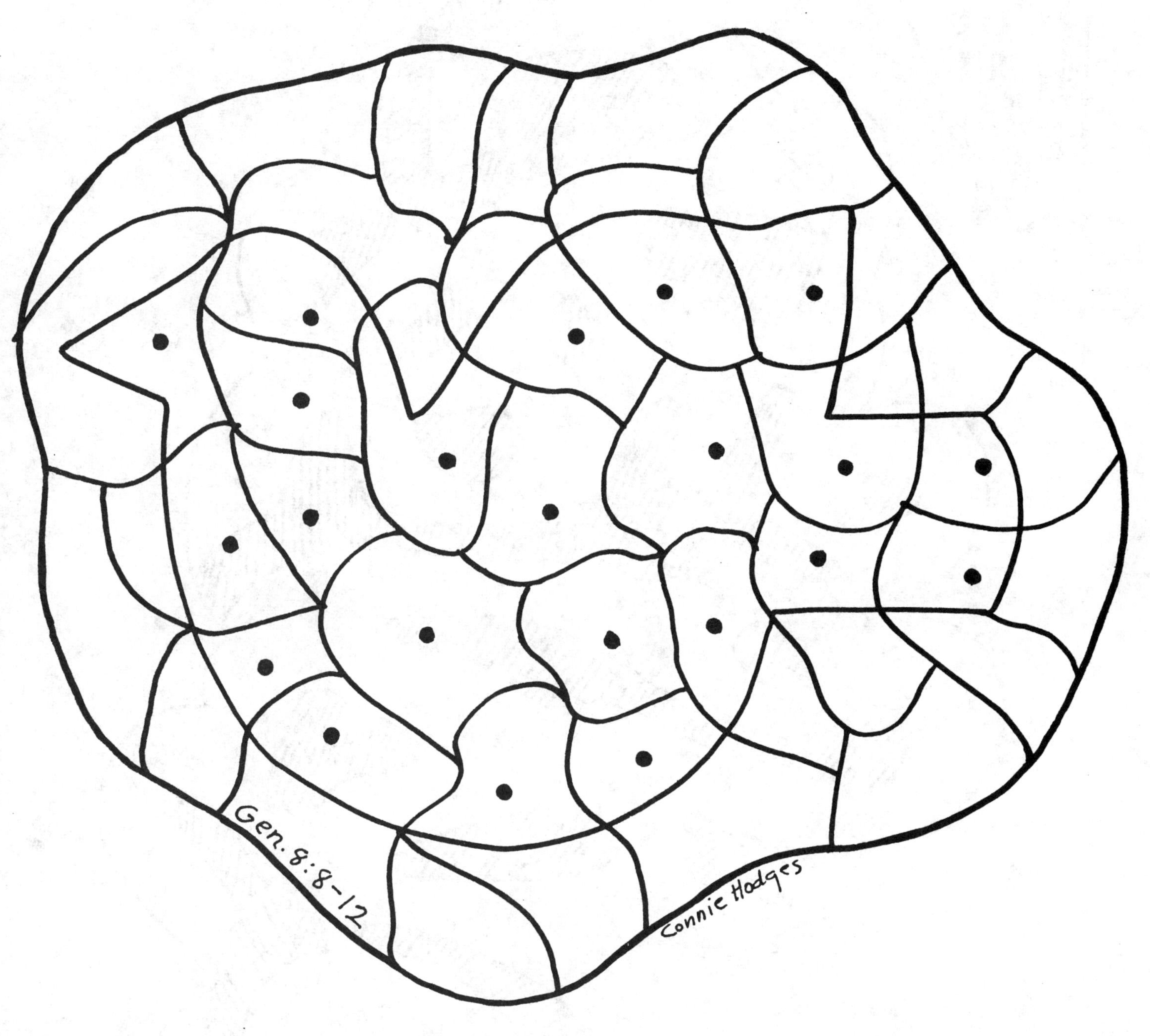

After the flooding and the dark,
Noah sent a dove from the ark.

Help Moses find his way up the mountain to receive the Ten Commandments.

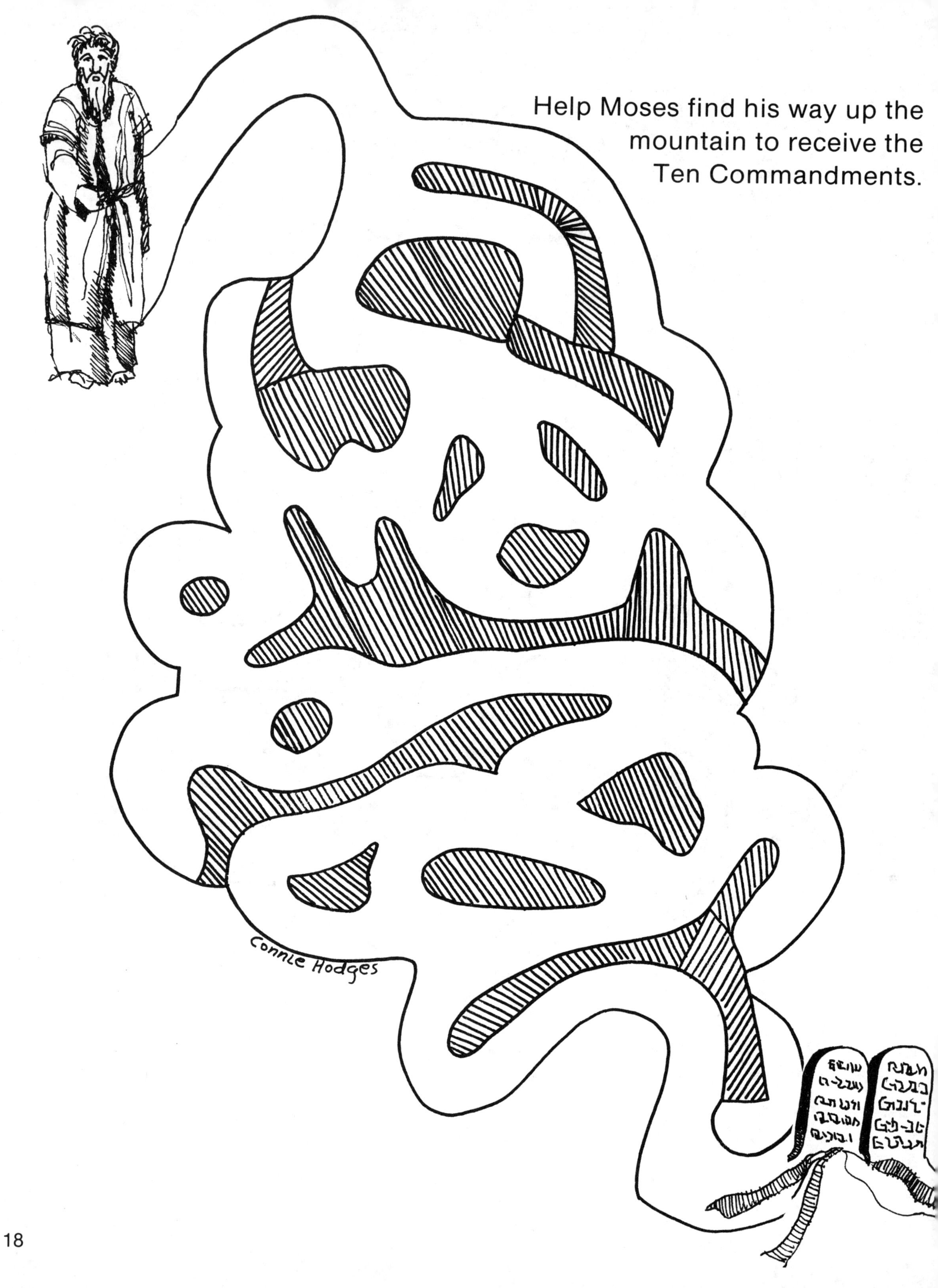

Fill in the blanks.

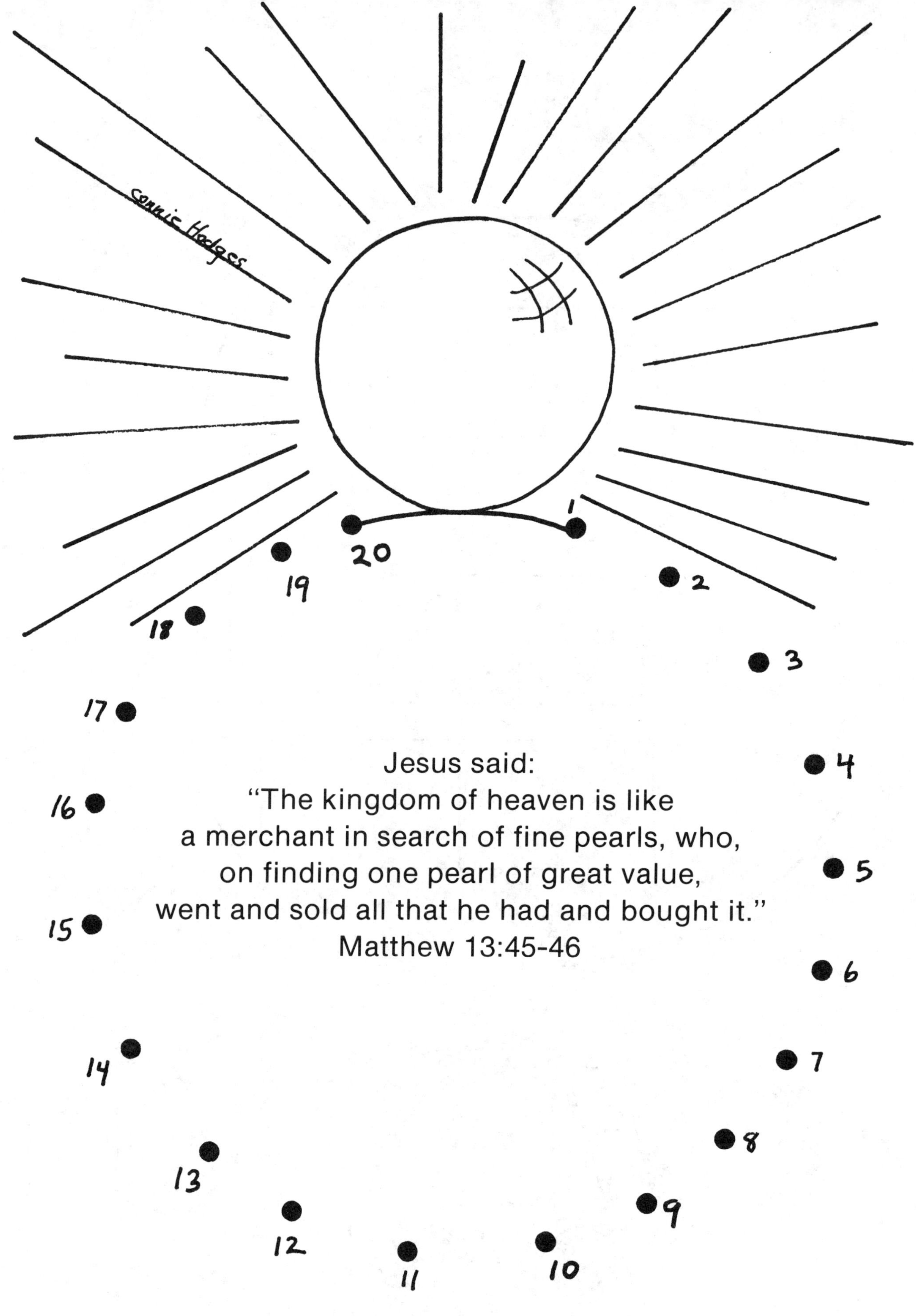

Jesus said:
"The kingdom of heaven is like
a merchant in search of fine pearls, who,
on finding one pearl of great value,
went and sold all that he had and bought it."
Matthew 13:45-46

Draw a line from each number to the next.

Help David escape to Naioth
1 Samuel 19:18

The Spirit of God appeared as a dove.
Draw a line from one number to the next.
Color the dove.

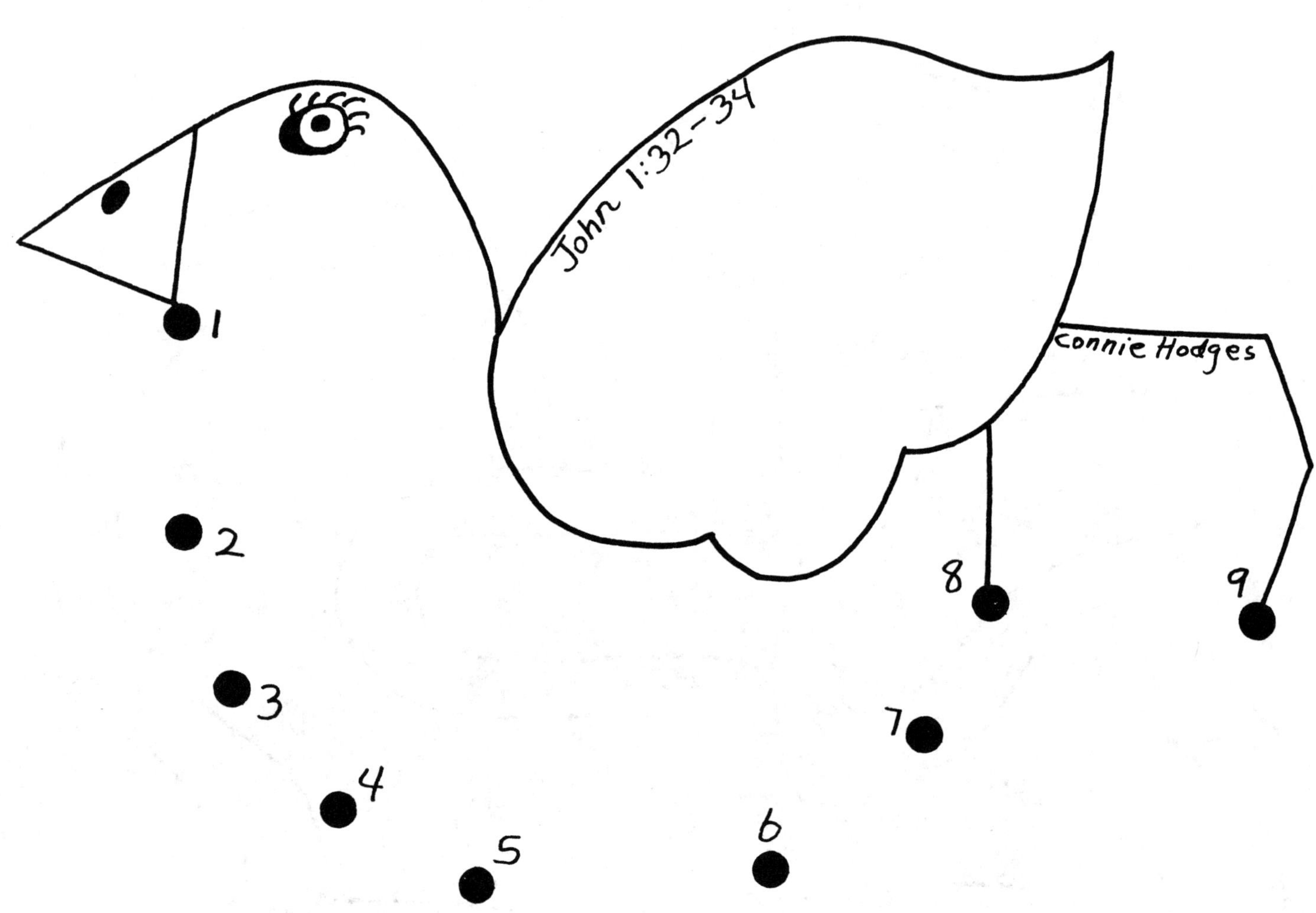

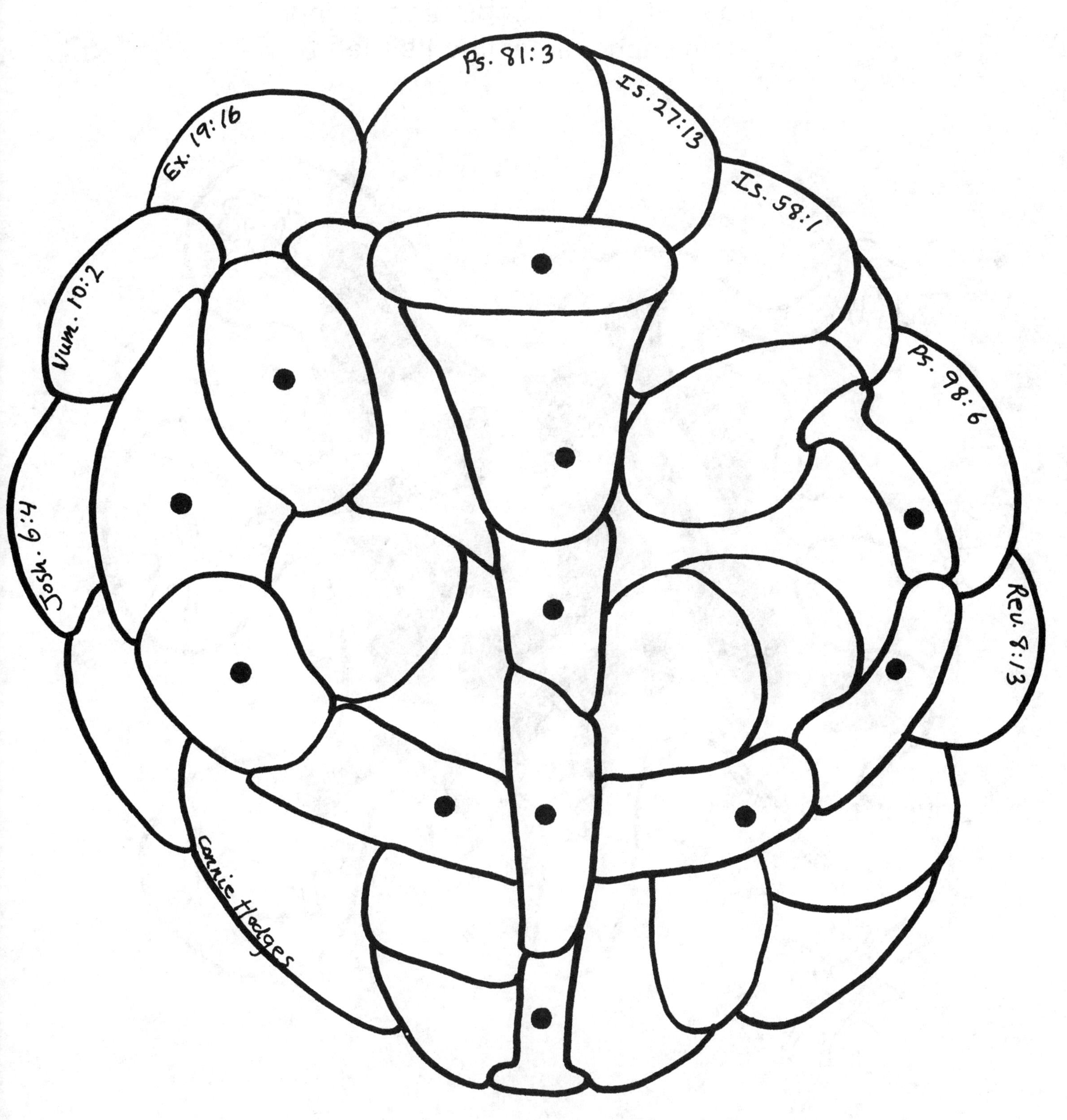

Fill in the places which have a dot in them.
"Lift up your voice like a trumpet."
Isaiah 58:1

Draw a line from beginning to end;
Help each animal find its friend.

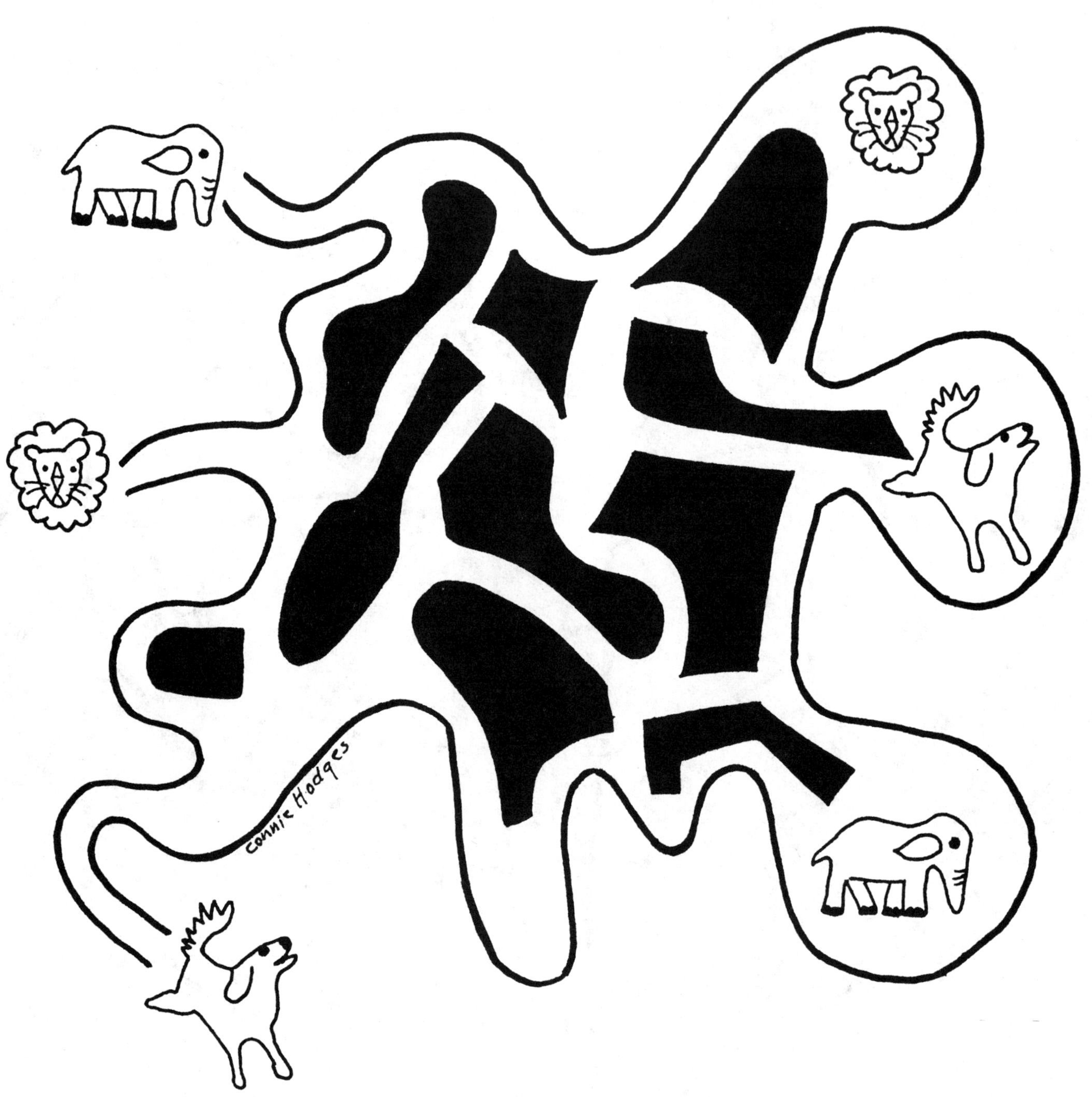

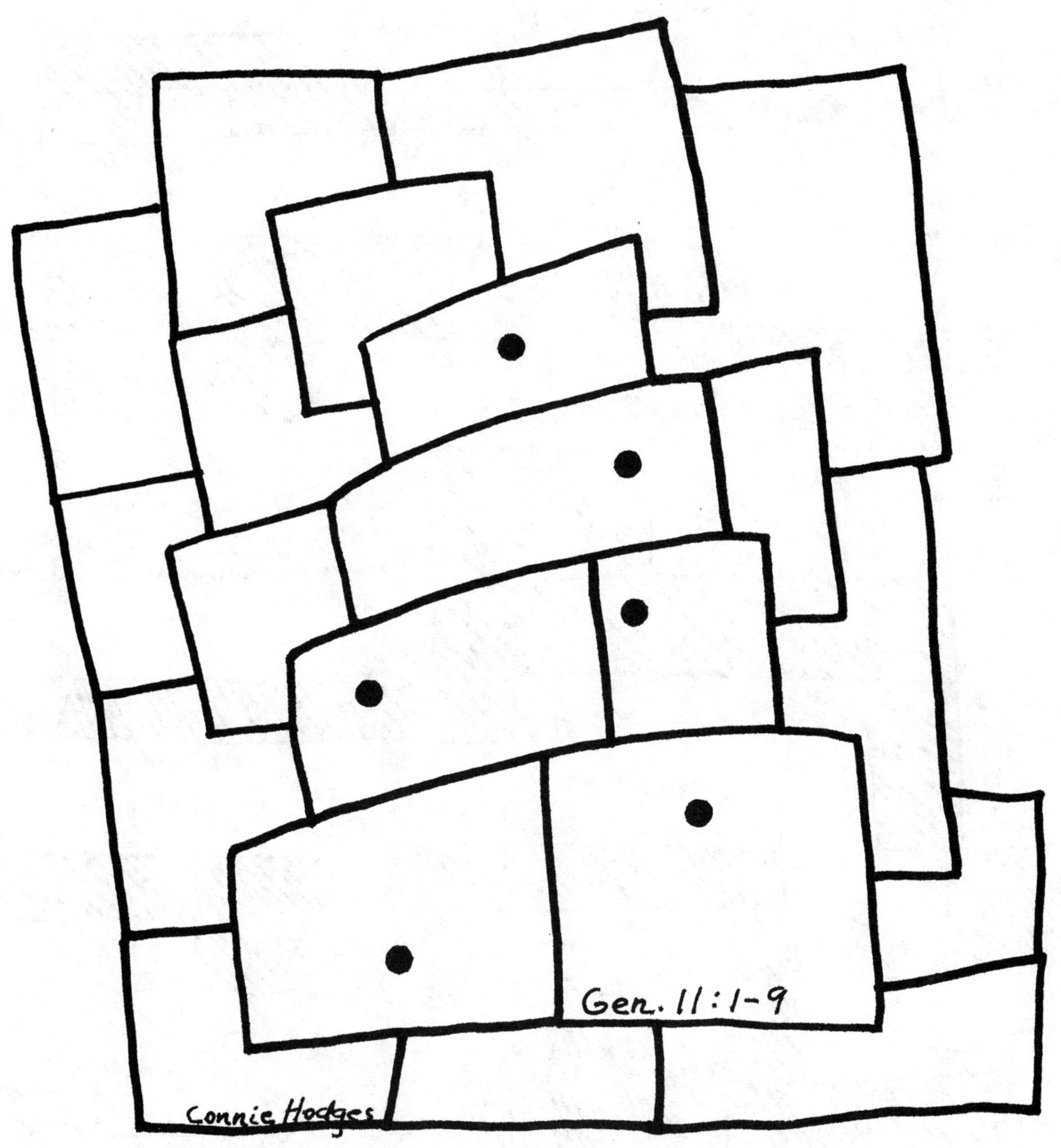

Color in each shape that has a dot in it.
Noah's children built a city called Babel,
and tried to build a tower so high
its top would reach heaven.

Help Mary and Joseph find
the way to Bethlehem.
Connie Hodges

Connect the dots
with lines from number
to number and you
will see the star
of Bethlehem!

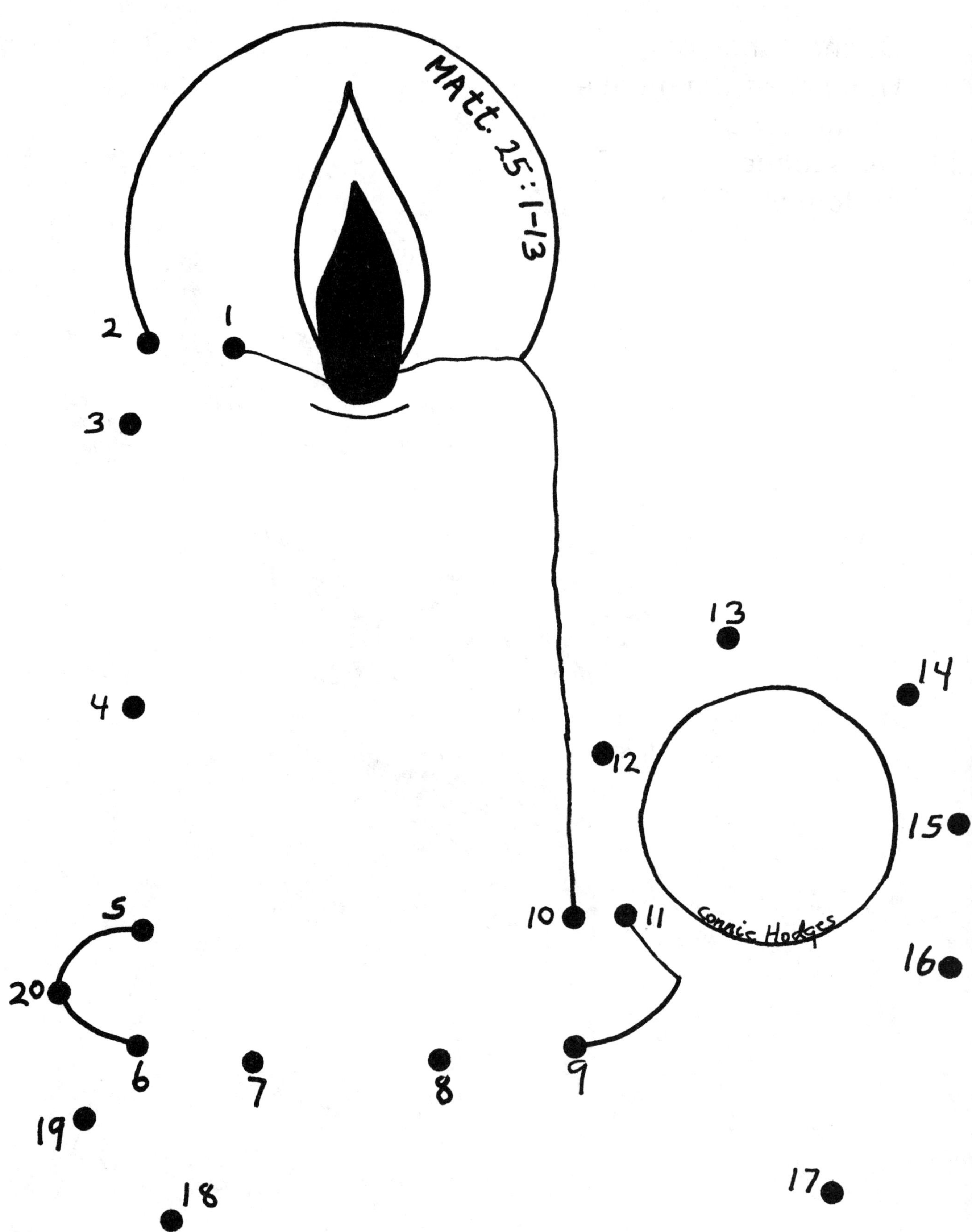

Draw a line from one number to the next.
Jesus wants us to *watch* and be ready for Him.

Fill in the blanks.

Jesus rode a donkey into Jerusalem.
The people shouted: "Hosanna!" John 12:1-19
Draw a line from one number to the next.

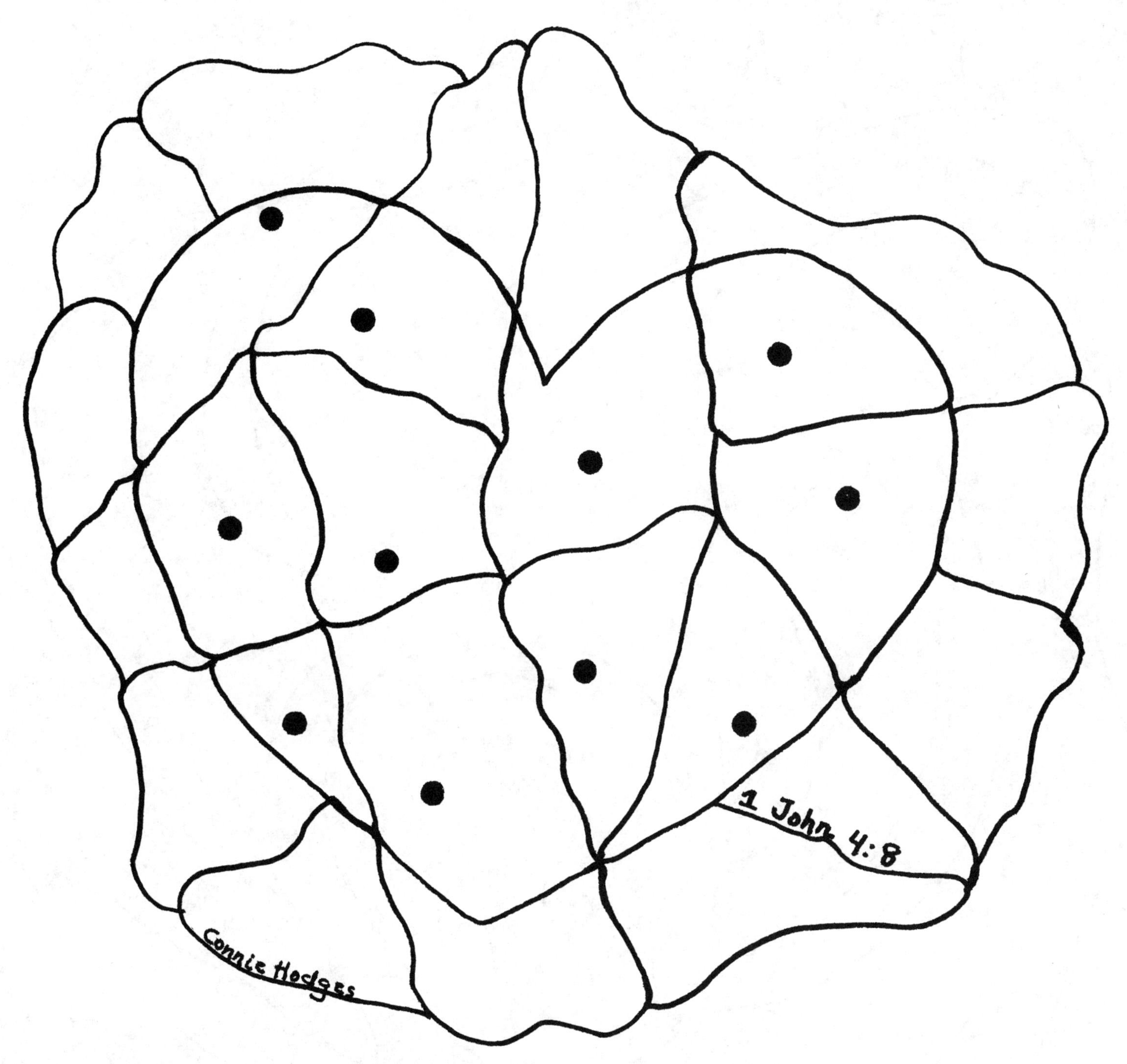

"God is Love."
Fill in the spaces that contain dots.
What do you see?

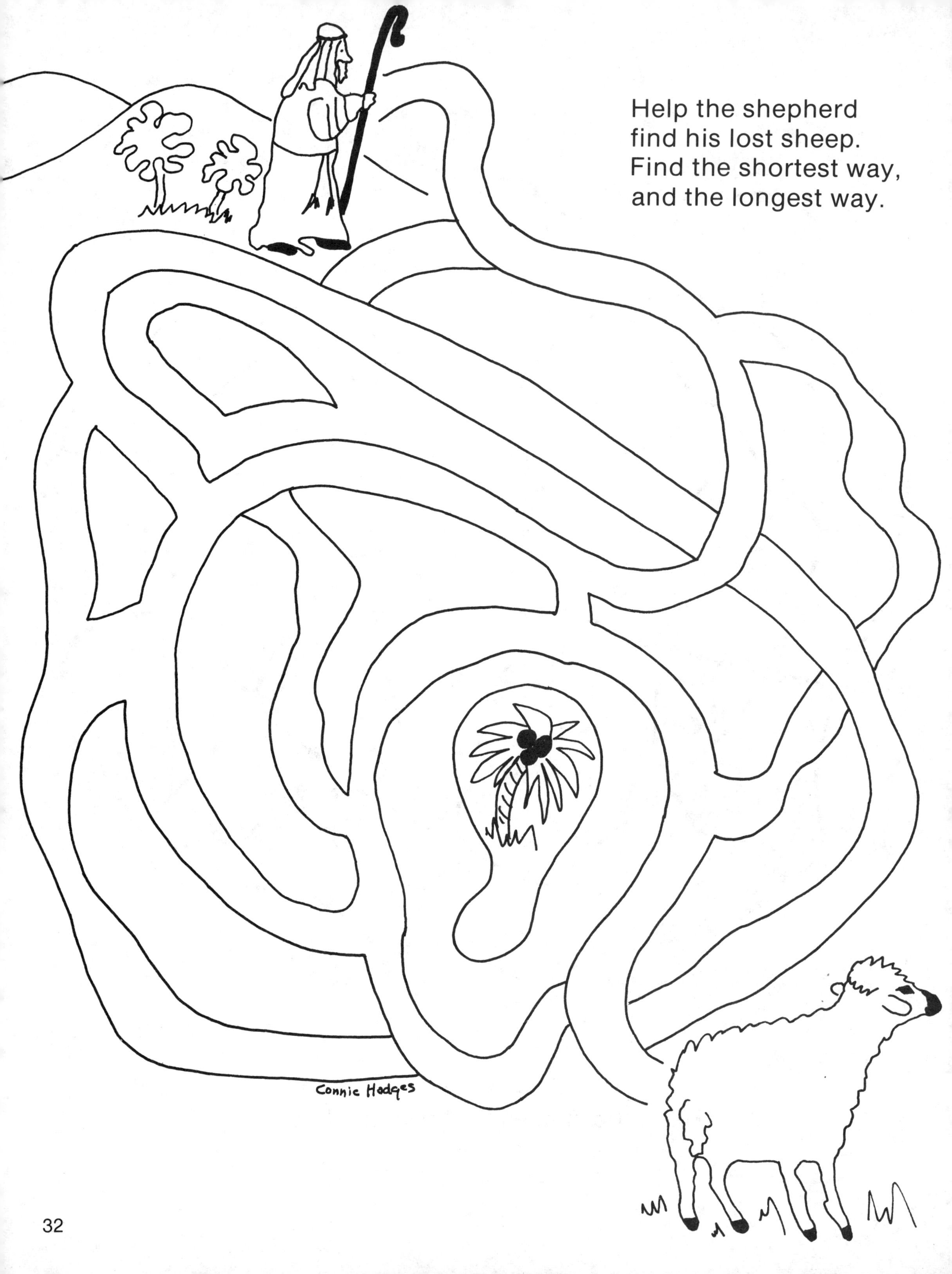
Help the shepherd
find his lost sheep.
Find the shortest way,
and the longest way.
Connie Hodges